I Surrender

SACRED PIANO ARRANGEMENTS FOR THE ADVANCED PIANIST

BY JONATHAN KURTZ

I Surrender...

Jonathan Kurtz has been arranging and composing music since childhood. He studied music education at Taylor University in Upland, IN and completed a Master of Arts degree in music at the University of Maryland. Jonathan resides in Middletown, MD with his wife Rachel and son James where he teaches middle school band and theatre arts in the Frederick County Public School system.

In our walks with God, complete surrender is probably one of the most difficult things we strive for. Letting go of what we seek to control through our own strength can only bring us closer to God and help us to hear His voice over our own desires. I pray that these arrangements may be used to quiet the soul and tune the ear to the precious whispers of the Holy Spirit. Since these arrangements are meant to be acts of worship, I have no expectation that they always be played in a certain way or the same way every time. God can say many things through one song, and His gift of music has the awesome ability to speak to us in ways that words cannot.

This book is dedicated to all of the music teachers I have had along the way. Your time and dedication to my success means so much and has made a major impact in my life. Thank you!

www.jonathankurtzmusic.com

Cover photos: Jonathan Kurtz
Graphic Design: Cara Boyer Photography. www.caraboyer.com

I Surrender

Arrangements by Jonathan Kurtz

The Deep Love of Jesus

And I pray that you, being rooted and established in love, 18 may have power, together with all the Lord's holy people, to grasp how wide and long and high and deep is the love of Christ,

Ephesians 3:18

Thomas J. Williams
Arr. by J. Kurtz

1

The Deep Love of Jesus

2

The Deep Love of Jesus

3

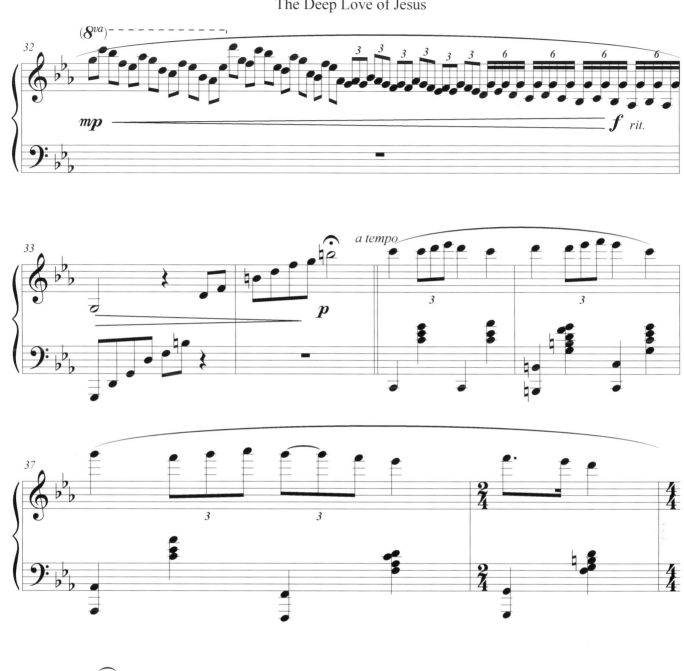

When I Survey...

They will look on the one they have pierced
John 19:37

Traditional
Arr. by Jonathan Kurtz

When I Survey

8

When I Survey

10

When I Survey

12

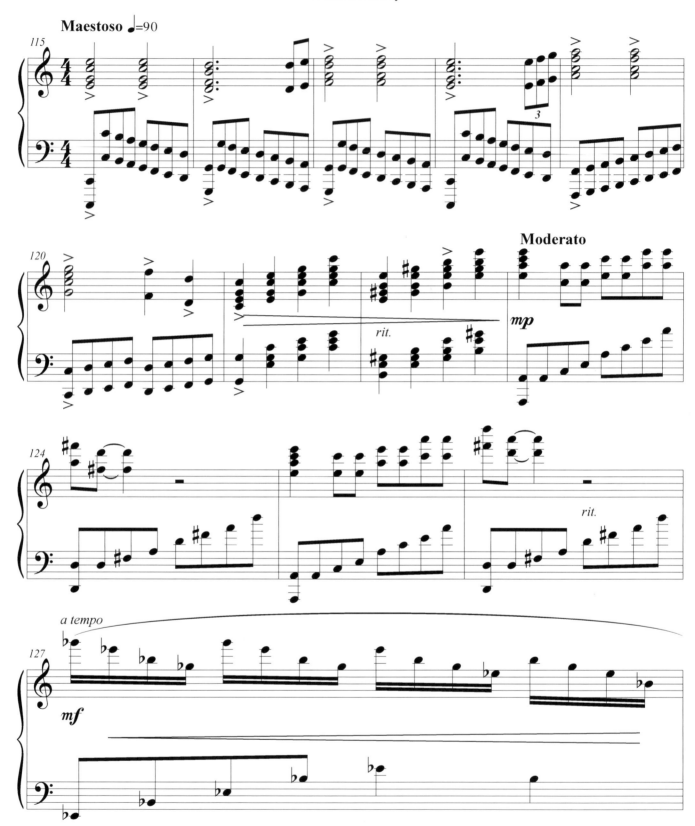

When I Survey

O Come All Ye Faithful

A voice of one calling:
"In the wilderness prepare the way for the Lord[a];
make straight in the desert a highway for our God.
Isaiah 40:3

John Francis Wade
Arr. byJonathan Kurtz

Delicate and Haunting
Moderato

O Come All Ye Faithful

18

O Come All Ye Faithful

O Come All Ye Faithful

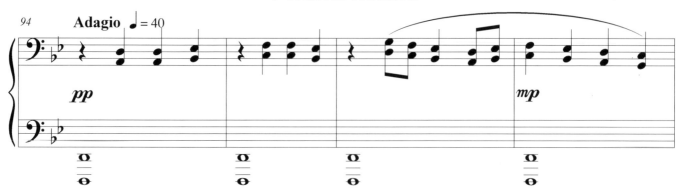

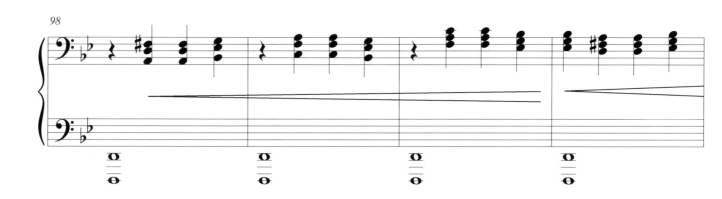

O Come All Ye Faithful

Give Me Jesus

What is more, I consider everything a loss compared to the
surpassing greatness of knowing Christ Jesus my Lord, for
whose sake I have lost all things. I consider them rubbish,
that I may gain Christ

Philippians 3:8

Traditional
Arr. by J. Kurtz

Give Me Jesus

24

Give Me Jesus

25

Give Me Jesus

Give Me Jesus

I Surrender All

I appeal to you therefore, brothers, by the mercies of God, to present
your bodies as a living sacrifice, holy and acceptable to God, which is
your spiritual worship.

~Romans 12:1

Winfield S. Weeden
Arr. by Jonathan Kurtz

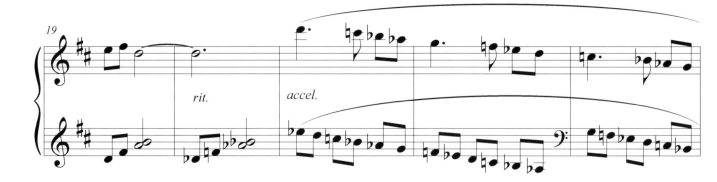

I Surrender All

30

I Surrender All

internal conflict that prevents complete surrender

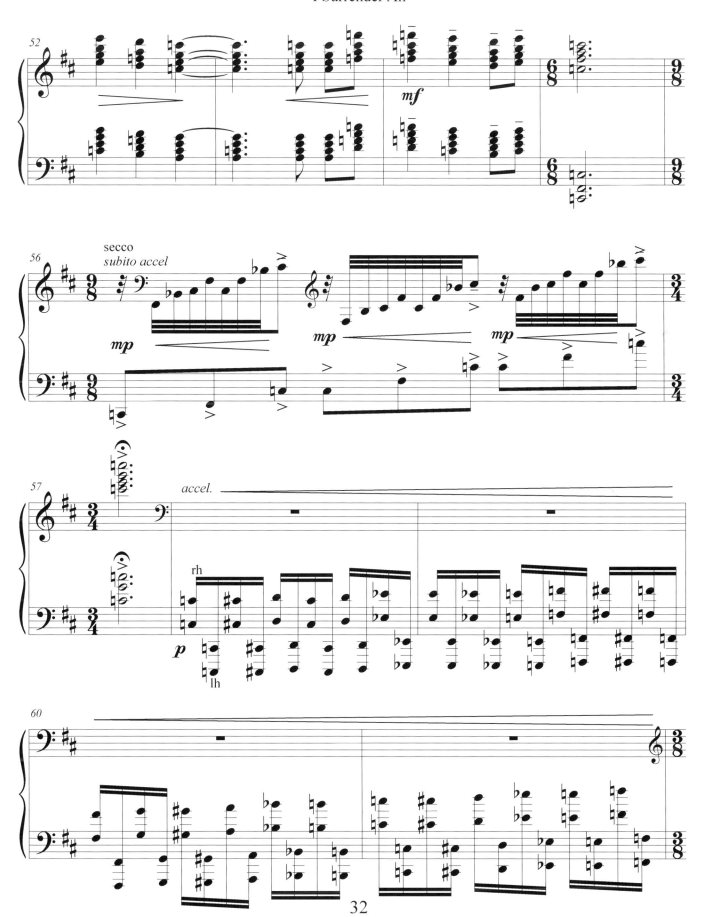

I Surrender All

33

I Surrender All

34

I Surrender All

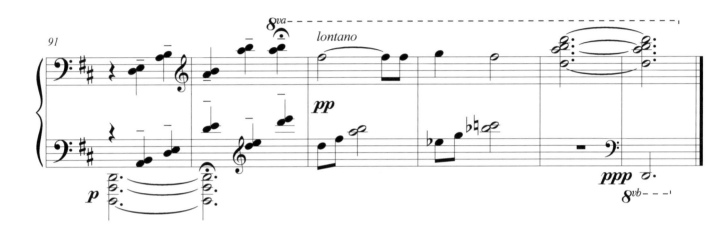

35

Love Divine, All Love Excelling

*His divine power has given to us all things that pertain to life and godliness,
through the knowledge of Him who called us by glory and virtue.*

2 Peter 1:3

**Wesley and Zundel
Arr. by J. Kurtz**

Love Divine, All Love Excelling

Love Divine, All Love Excelling

Love Divine, All Love Excelling

All Hail the Power of Jesus' Name

"You are worthy our Lord and God
to receive glory and honor and power,
For you created all things,
And by your will they were created,
And have their being."
Rev 4:11

Oliver Holden
Arr. by Jonathan Kurtz

All Hail the Power of Jesus' Name

All Hail the Power of Jesus' Name

All Hail the Power of Jesus' Name

All Hail the Power of Jesus' Name

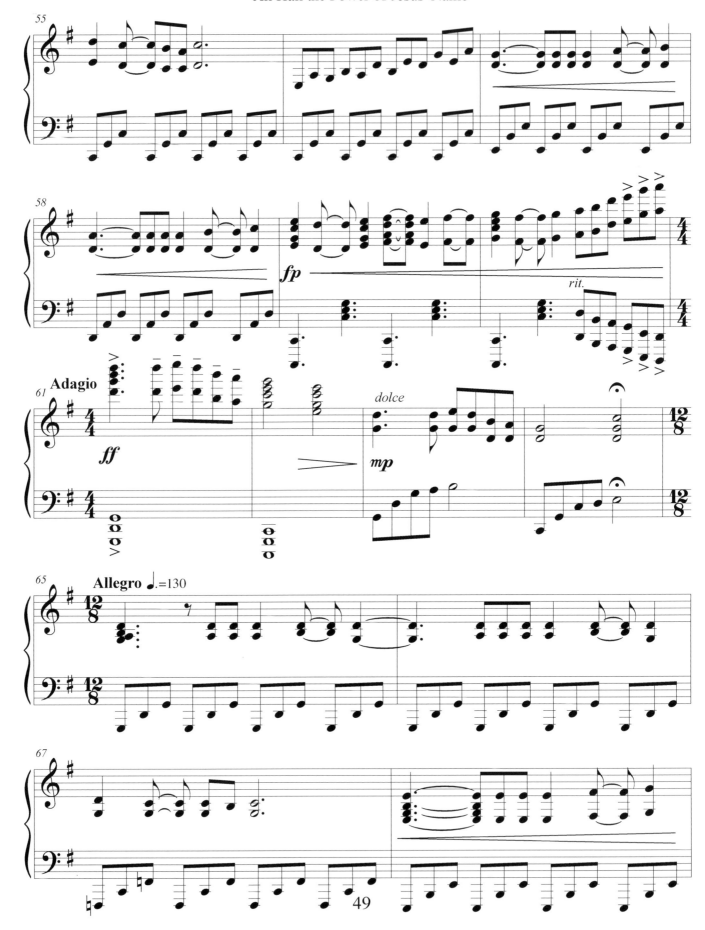

All Hail the Power of Jesus' Name

At the Cross

For the message of the cross is foolishness to those
who are perishing, but to us who are being saved it is the power of God.

I Corinthians 1:18

Ralph E. Hudson
Arr. by J. Kurtz

In the distance ♩= 62

At the Cross

At the Cross

Washed and Paid

If we confess our sins, He is faithful and just and will forgive us our sins and
purify us from all unrighteousness.

I John 1:9

John T. Grape
Arr. by Jonathan Kurtz

56

Washed and Paid

57

Washed and Paid

Washed and Paid

60

Fantasia on Come Thou Long Expected Jesus

Therefore the Lord Himself will give you a sign: Behold, the virgin shall conceive and bear a Son, and shall call His name Immanuel.

Isaiah 7:14

Rowland H. Prichard
Arranged by J Kurtz

Fantasy on Come Thou Long Expected Jesus

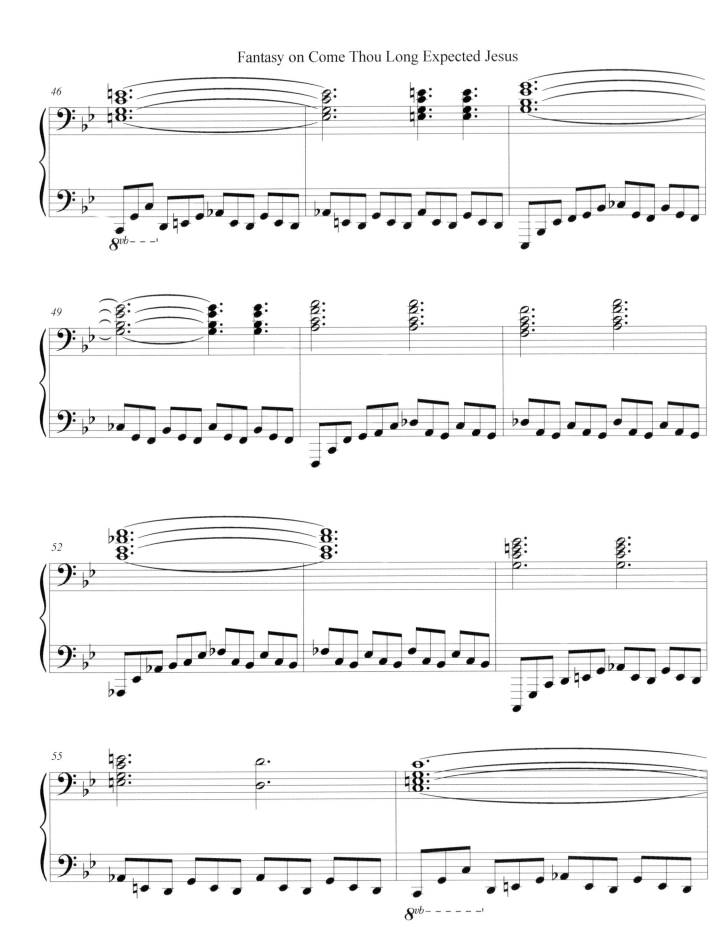

Fantasy on Come Thou Long Expected Jesus

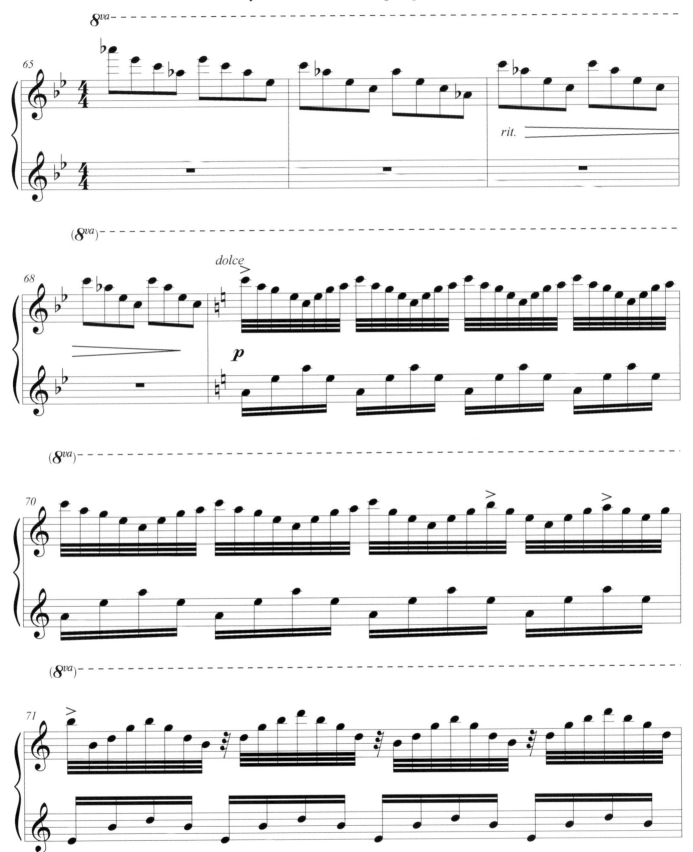

Fantasy on Come Thou Long Expected Jesus

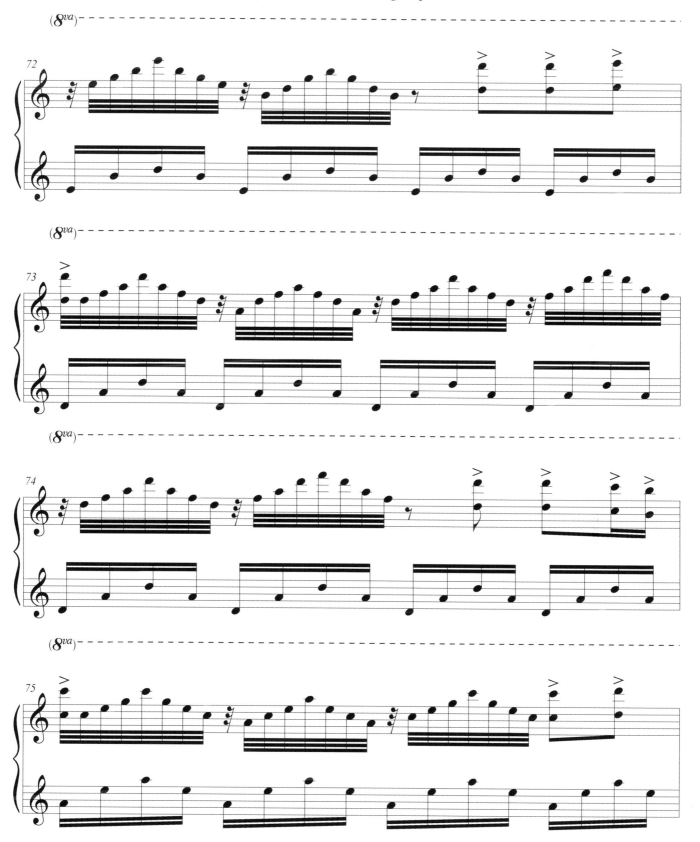

68

Fantasy on Come Thou Long Expected Jesus

70

Fantasy on Come Thou Long Expected Jesus

71

Made in the USA
Columbia, SC
30 September 2023

23670859R00043